# The Stock Market

*What It Is and How It Works*

ECONOMICS
*in the* 21st
CENTURY

# The Stock Market

## *What It Is and How It Works*

Lisa A. Crayton and Kathy Furgang

**Enslow Publishing**
101 W. 23rd Street
Suite 240
New York, NY 10011
USA
enslow.com

Published in 2016 by Enslow Publishing, LLC.
101 W. 23rd Street, Suite 240, New York, NY 10011

**Library of Congress Cataloging-in-Publication Data**

Crayton, Lisa A., author.
  The stock market : what it is and how it works / Lisa A. Crayton and Kathy Furgang.
    pages cm. -- (Economics in the 21st century)
  Includes bibliographical references and index.
  ISBN 978-0-7660-7384-5
  1. Stock exchanges--Juvenile literature. 2. Investments--Juvenile literature. 3. Speculation--Juvenile
literature. 4. Finance--Juvenile literature. I. Furgang, Kathy, author. II. Title.
  HG4553.C73 2016
  332.64'2--dc23
                                        2015031230

Printed in the United States of America

**To Our Readers:** We have done our best to make sure all website addresses in this book were active and appropriate when we went to press. However, the author and the publisher have no control over and assume no liability for the material available on those websites or on any websites they may link to. Any comments or suggestions can be sent by e-mail to customerservice@enslow.com.

Portions of this text were originally written by Kathy Furgang.

**Photos Credits:** Cover, AshDesign/Shutterstock.com (left), Syda Productions/Shutterstock.com (center), Songquan Deng/Shutterstock.com (right); p. 6 Jeff Greenberg 6 of 6/Alamy; p. 9 Andrew Burton/Getty Images News/Getty Images; p. 10 Hulton Archive/Archive Photos/Getty Images; p. 11 Ben Hider/Getty Images Entertainment/Getty Images; p. 13 Mario Tama/Getty Images North America/Getty Images; p. 15 Michael Nagle/Bloomberg/Getty Images; p. 17 Ben Hider/Getty Images Entertainment/Getty Images; p. 18 Emmanuel Dunand/AFP/Getty Image; p. 23 Tim Graham/Getty Images News/Getty Images; p. 25 Joseph Sohm/Shutterstock.com; p. 30 Portland Press Herald/Getty Images; p. 32 iStock.com/Monkey Business Images; p. 34 iStock.com/Tupungato; p. 39 Hulton Archive/Getty Images; p. 40 Yuriko Nakao/Bloomberg/Getty Images; p. 42 Martin Divisek/Bloomberg/Getty Images; p. 44 Universal History Archive/Universal Images Group/Getty Images; p. 47 Popperfoto/Getty Images; p. 49 OFF/AFP/Getty Images; p. 51 FSA/Archive Photos/Getty Images; p. 53 Universal History Archive/Universal Images Group/Getty Images; p. 55 Al Gould/Interim Archives/Archive Photos/Getty Images; p. 59 Burlingham/Shutterstock.com; p. 61 iStock.com/Oktay Ortakcioglu; p. 62 Spencer Platt/Getty Images News/Getty Images; p. 63 Justin Sullivan/Getty Images North America/Getty Images; p. 66 Photo by Kristoffer Tripplaar-Pool/Getty Images News/ Getty Images; p. 68 Kzenon/Shutterstock.com; 70 John Moore/Getty Images News/Getty News; p. 72 John Greim/LightRocket/Getty Images; p. 74 Serr Novick/Thinkstock; p. 75 iStock.com/Hocus-Focus; p. 77 Christopher Furlong/Getty Images News/Getty Images; p. 78 Mario Tama/Getty Images News/Getty Images; p. 79 Mario Tama/Getty Images News/Getty Images.

# Contents

Whether online, on television, or in print, news reports contain a lot of information about the stock market and are a common way for students to learn about it.

# CHAPTER 1

# *Vital Economic Engine*

The stock market is a familiar topic to many students. Some learn about it in a financial literacy class that teaches students about basic money management principles, along with information on investing. Others learn about the stock market in US history class where discussions focus on the stock market crash of 1929. Yet others are privy to family members' conversations about the good—or bad—impact recent stock activity has had on their retirement accounts or other investments.

Did you learn about stocks from any of those avenues? Or, are you most familiar with another common source of stock market information: news reports. News about the stock market abounds—in print and online. Usually, stocks' performances are discussed in terms of their ups and downs, activity that's sometimes difficult to understand. Often, people will skip over these reports, believing the news is only important to investors. Not so! The stock market greatly impacts the economy and therefore affects all of us. That's why it is important to become *more* knowledgeable about what a stock market is and how it works.

## What Is the Stock Market?

The stock market is a place that sells stocks. A stock is a partial ownership of a company. Buying stocks is attractive to people because investors can potentially make money—sometimes lots of it—if stocks go up. The bad news is that they can also lose money—sometimes a tremendous amount or all of their invested money—if the stocks go down. This happens because investing is risky. There are no guarantees about whether the stock market will do well overall or if one company's stock will perform well over time. No one likes losing money, so why invest in the stock market? Again, it's because of the many opportunities for people to make a lot of money. These opportunities are what have kept the stock market a vital engine for the economy and American business and industry for more than a century.

We have all seen the following chaotic scene on TV or in the movies: People dressed in suits rush across a crowded floor, chatter on phones, and yell back and forth to each other as they wave little pieces of paper in the air. All the while, they glance up at numbers that flash on computer screens and electronic scrolls that surround them. This scene depicts the stock market at work. The people you see running around are working at a stock exchange. They are helping people all around the world buy and sell stocks, which are ownership shares of companies.

When someone owns one or more shares of a company, he or she is known as a shareholder. This person becomes part owner of that company. Anyone who puts his or her money into the stock market by buying shares of companies is called an investor. An investor hopes to make a profit with his or her investment. There are many opportunities to make money in the stock market. If a company does well, its profits go up and shareholders

The people seen hustling busily all over the floor of the exchange are known as stockbrokers. They buy and sell shares of companies for their investors.

make money. However, if a company does not do well and its profits slow or decrease, a shareholder may lose money.

The people who run around the stock exchange floor are called stockbrokers. They work all day to help people buy or sell shares of companies. Suppose a company is selling its shares for $10 each. An investor might want to buy ten shares. So he or she pays $100 and then owns a very small portion of the company. The investor may make more money than he or she spent on the stock purchase if the company does well and makes a profit. A company that sells shares of its company to the public is called a public company. Companies "go public" and sell stock in order to raise more money to operate—to hire more employees, to expand operations, and to research and develop new products.

# Financial Center of the United States

The financial center of the US economy is located at the southern tip of the island of Manhattan on a narrow lane called Wall Street. This is the site of the New York Stock Exchange (NYSE). In this building is where most stock buying and selling is done in the United States. This constant buying and selling of stocks is called trading.

The history of Wall Street goes back almost four hundred years, long before there was even a nation known as the United States. Dutch explorers and colonists settled Manhattan back in 1625. (*Manhattan* comes from a Lenape word meaning "island of many hills.") They called the place New Amsterdam. It was part of New Netherland, a Dutch colony stretching from Cape Cod in the north to the Delmarva Peninsula in the south. In 1653, the Dutch built

This is an image from about 1796, looking toward
Wall Street in New York City's financial area.

Today the New York Stock Exchange is still located on Wall Street.
It's one of the largest economic marketplaces in the world.

a 12-foot (3.66-meter) wooden wall in lower Manhattan that spanned from the East River to the Hudson River. The wall was intended as protection against Native Americans as well as the British. In 1685, after the wall was torn down, Wall Street was built running parallel to where the defensive wall originally stood.

From the beginning, Wall Street was a central meeting place for merchants who wished to trade commodities. Commodities are goods that have not been processed yet, such as wheat, tobacco, or cotton. Even slaves just arrived from Africa on slave ships were traded on Wall Street, which was near the city's port and large harbor.

Almost a century later, after Britain had seized control of Manhattan and the entire New York Colony from the Dutch, the thirteen colonies began to chafe under British rule. Rebellions began to break out, and lower Manhattan was a common place for protest. During the Revolutionary War, hundreds of houses along Wall Street were burned down, most likely by patriots who did not want to surrender the city to the British.

In 1792, following the American Revolution, a group of twenty-four brokers decided to form a group devoted to the selling of public stocks. They would be paid by other people to trade stocks for them. The brokers signed an agreement under a buttonwood tree at 68 Wall Street and continued to do their work there for years, moving to a coffeehouse in the winter. The document they signed, known as the Buttonwood Agreement, formed the first formal New York stock exchange. In 1817, the organization created a constitution and was officially renamed the New York Stock and Exchange Board. Today, this organization is simply known as the New York Stock Exchange. That same year, operations moved to a rented room ($200/ month) at 40 Wall Street.

The NYSE's floor is almost always bustling with busy brokers, buying and trading.

Brokers had to belong to the New York Stock Exchange in order to do business there. That did not stop outside brokers from earning money on their own, however. These outside brokers traded securities right on the street corners of Wall Street. Securities are certificates of stocks that prove a person's partial ownership in a company.

## Understanding Capitalism

Can the public be part owners of companies in any area around the world? Do all countries sell and trade shares in their public companies? Most of them do, but not all. The system that allows the United States and many other countries to trade and sell goods and shares of companies is called capitalism. According to the ideas of capitalism, anyone has the right to manufacture and sell goods for a profit. American companies can make more money to help develop, run, and expand their businesses by getting public support in the form of cash investments. They might use the funds raised through sales of stocks to hire more workers, build new factories, develop new or improved products, or simply pocket the profits and get richer. A company that does not pass along some of the profits to its shareholders, however, or funnel profits back into business operations and development probably won't remain successful for long.

The stocks of companies that manufacture and sell products or services that are in high demand usually rise. More people are interested in these companies because they are developing popular products or services, selling a lot of units, and making a lot of money. Companies that do not have a successful product may find that their stock prices are dropping. People are not willing to take a risk and invest in that company if they don't feel their profits are rising and

# Focus on Fitness

Whatever your interest, you can find a stock tied to a particular product or company. If fitness is your arena of interest, for example, the sporting goods company Nike and GNC, a supplier of vitamins and related natural products, are just two companies publicly traded on the stock market.

In June 2015, Fitbit, Inc. became another with its initial public offering (IPO). The company manufactures Fitbit, a fitness product that allows users to track their exercise routines, including the number of daily steps. Worn on the body or on

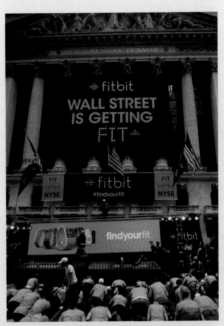

Trainer Harley Pasternak and actress Jordana Brewster are on hand to help celebrate the initial public offering (IPO) for Fitbit.

clothing, the product has received rave reviews from health-conscious consumers. By September 2015, its performance had been mixed, with an initial encouraging surge followed by a drastic plunge. As autumn approached, its stock began to climb again, but only time will tell if this or any stock also is a good fit for investors and whether it enjoys strong performance.

their products are good or desirable. The supply and demand of a company's stock often corresponds to that of the goods or services the company offers. If demand for a company's products is high, its stock tends to be in high demand, too. So the stock price rises. The opposite is true for a company whose products and services are not in high demand among consumers.

In today's markets, people buy and sell goods that are made in all areas of the world by American and foreign companies. This is called a global market. Investors may buy or sell stocks all around the world, too. Foreign investors can buy stock in American companies, and American investors can purchase shares in publicly traded foreign businesses. The New York Stock Exchange is not the only one in the world. There are more than fifty major stock exchanges worldwide, on every continent except Antarctica.

## Key Indexes

Though not the only stock exchange, the New York Stock Exchange is the largest in the world in terms of market value. It is second largest in terms of the volume of transactions, behind the National Association of Securities Dealers Automated Quotations (NASDAQ). The NASDAQ is also based in New York. Each year, trillions of dollars of stock trade through the NYSE on four trading room floors. Brokers do the buying and selling at the direction of their customers, who place orders. Several basic ways in which an investor can keep track of how the stock market is performing exist. There are three popular indexes that people can check to review stock results. They are the NASDAQ, the Dow Jones Industrial Average (often referred to as "the Dow Jones" or "the Dow"), and the Standard and Poor's 500 (the S&P 500).

The NASDAQ, founded in 1971, is important for both brokers and investors. It is an electronic stock exchange where brokers can buy and sell stocks

The National Association of Securities Dealers Automated Quotations (NASDAQ) welcomes Facebook as it begins its first day of trading.

This electronic board shows onlookers whether their stocks' prices are moving up and making money or falling and losing value.

# Stockbrokers Street Talk

Stockbrokers must be able to communicate prices to each other in order to buy and sell stocks. In the early 1800s, messengers raced back and forth between brokerage houses with handwritten orders to buy and sell stocks. Sharing information with stock exchanges in other cities was more difficult. Men used flags to signal the prices of stocks. People set up along an intercity route used telescopes to read, record, and pass on this information to the next person along the route. Both of these methods were replaced with Morse code once Samuel Morse invented the telegraph in 1838.

By 1867, the ticker tape machine was invented. This allowed all of the brokerage houses to get the same information at the same time along a long strip of paper called a ticker tape. A clerk would then write the stock prices on a board for everyone to see. Eventually, this method was replaced with electronic displays. Today, stock prices instantly flash on television, computer, and cell phone screens around the world. There are even huge scrolling electronic tickers in public places, like New York City's Times Square.

via computer. About thirty-eight thousand companies trade their securities through this exchange. It has more trading volume per hour than any other exchange in the world.

The NASDAQ is an index as well as a stock exchange. A stock index is a measurement of the performance of a sample collection of companies' stocks, usually the stocks of the largest companies traded in that exchange. When the news reports that "the NASDAQ gained one hundred points today," that means the collective value of the stocks chosen for its index went up by that number of points. When the point value of the NASDAQ is reported, a percentage gain or loss is also reported. This is a more important indicator of how the stock market did that day. It may have gained 2 percent or lost 1.5 percent of its cumulative value (the total worth of the stock of the companies in the index). These numbers let investors know if the stock market as a whole is gaining or losing value, because the companies in the index are taken to be representative of the larger economy.

Business news reports often state that "the Dow was up today" or "the Dow Jones took a hit today." The Dow Jones Industrial Average is another kind of index, or reference point, that gives an overall sense of how the stock market is doing. There is no way to quickly report the results of every company during the day, so the Dow is an average of the thirty most widely held and largest companies in the United States. The Dow does not indicate how every company that is traded on the NYSE performed. It is simply an average of some of the biggest of them.

The S&P 500 is another index for reporting stock averages. It is an index of five hundred companies, the largest ones holding a greater weight on the index than the smaller ones.

# CHAPTER 2
# *The Stock Market in Action*

U p. Down. Up. Down. The economy moves through various stages of growth—or expansion—and contraction. These stages impact the stock market. They also affect investors' ability to sell and buy stocks. When the economy is strong and growing, it is said to be in a period of prosperity. People benefit from an investing environment that makes it relatively easy to make money in the stock market. The good atmosphere also affects consumer confidence, especially as hiring and salaries increase and companies' profits rise.

That prosperity comes to a halt when the economy starts sliding into a new phase: recession. This downturn is, again, a normal part of the economy. Unlike the beneficial conditions prevalent during a period of prosperity, however, the recession ushers in tough financial times. People, business, cities, and states are impacted by the slowing economy. Demand for goods and services drop. This results in fewer company profits and prompts job and salary cuts. As the recession deepens, the impact spirals throughout the economy. You may recall that is exactly what happened during the recent recession from 2007–2009.

## Ripple Effects

Like throwing a stone into a pond, a recession can have a ripple effect on many other parts of the economy. When companies need fewer workers, they must lay people off in order to continue to make a profit. At the same time, they are making fewer goods because consumer demand has gone down, in part because of insecurity over the economy. Laid-off workers will have less money to spend in their everyday lives because they no longer get a regular paycheck. They will not be able to buy new goods such as cars, TVs, clothing, and furniture. They will have less money to go to the movies, restaurants, and amusement parks.

The more companies that lay off people during a recession, the more people there are who cannot keep the economy running through consumer spending. Eventually, people who have been laid off may not be able to pay their rent or their mortgages. Even those workers who hang on to their jobs may be so worried about being laid off in the near future that they cut way back on their household spending and begin to save money instead.

What happens when fewer people are spending money in a slow economy? The economy slows even more. The companies that let go of workers are now selling even fewer goods than before. So they make even smaller profits (or no profits at all) and may have to lay off even more workers. The companies' falling stock prices reflect their poor performance. As a result, investors in these companies are no longer making any money. They may begin to lose confidence in the companies they have invested their money in. Investors may sell their stock, and those companies then have even less money to help them get through the difficult times. Some companies can no longer make a profit and may fail altogether, declaring bankruptcy and going out of business.

When a company lays off workers, this affects other parts of the economy, such as other businesses. Without a regular paycheck, people spend less money on luxury items, for example.

The more businesses that slow down, the more people are affected throughout the economy at all income levels—rich, poor, and middle class. It can take months or even years, but the ripple effects of a recession can reach specific regions of the country, the nation at large, and even the world markets.

## Keep or Sell?

Retail sales is one example of how company stocks are impacted during different economic climates. During a recession, decreased demand for a retailer's merchandise results in fewer sales and may lead to a store closing and affect company stocks. When the economy picks up, other factors may play a role. Slow sales, in part due to online shopping, for example, compelled the Gap, Inc. to announce another round of store closures in June 2015. The result: the price of its shares fell by eight cents. As of mid-June 2015, the retailer had experienced a 9 percent drop in its share prices, and as of early August its price had dropped lower than the June price. Every investor must choose how much risk to take on. If you were a Gap shareholder, would you still hold on to your stock, or would those drops make you anxious to sell?

## Downward Spiral

What causes an economic slowdown in the first place? Many things can bring it about. But often it's the period of prosperity itself that indirectly causes an eventual slowdown. All of the companies that are involved in making the goods and services sold to consumers will be doing great. If the companies are public, their stocks will likely be soaring and their investors will be happy that they are making money. The companies themselves will probably need to take on extra workers to keep up with the extra production needed to meet the increased demand for products and services. Hiring and salaries will probably increase. During a time when people have extra money to spend, they may decide to make "big ticket," or major, purchases like a new car or a vacation home.

But how many extra cars and homes can people buy? How long can company stocks soar as people buy these new products? The unusually high

When people have extra money to spend, they are more apt to buy more expensive items, such as cars.

demand for a particular good or service is often called a bubble. But what happens to bubbles after a while? They burst. Like any other bubble, goods and services bubbles eventually burst. This means there suddenly won't be a great demand for the products that people bought in good economic times. The companies will need to produce fewer of these products. As a result, they will need to employ fewer workers. Unemployed workers or employees who fear unemployment will drastically cut their spending, resulting in still lower levels of product production, more layoffs, and even less consumer spending. This will cause a downward spiral throughout the economy that keeps worsening as time goes on.

Not all bubbles burst, however. Sometimes demand remains high, even if it slows a bit, and technological advancement and innovative product development can keep consumer appetites whetted. For example, during the first half of the twentieth century, there was a great demand for telephones. Families were just beginning to buy their first home phones. Previously, most telephones were in offices or public places like drug stores. Workers laid more phone wires to accommodate the rising demand for home phones. Phone wires eventually stretched from one end of the country to the other. Telephone company stocks rose, and investors saw the industry as a worthy investment.

But what happened once everyone finally had a phone installed in his or her home? The telephone bubble did not burst. Technology kept improving, and people would eventually replace their old and outdated phones with new and better ones. The price of phones even dropped because so many people demanded them. They became so affordable that people eventually began to buy more than one phone for their homes. Then cell phones were introduced in the late-twentieth century, entirely reinvigorating the industry and stoking renewed consumer enthusiasm.

## What Are Bull and Bear Markets?

Experienced investors know that the stock market will always go through periods of prosperity and periods of slow growth (or even zero or negative growth). The term used to describe a period of faster growth and prosperity is *bull market.* Like a bull, the market charges on, strong and fierce. During a bull market, stock prices rise and investors make a lot of money. Soon more and more investors see their colleagues making money and decide they want in on the action, too. So they pour more and more money into the stock market, hoping for similarly big returns on their investment.

A period of economic slowdown is called a bear market. It is thought that the term dates back to the time when traders sold valuable bearskins. These skins were sold during periods in which traders feared that the prices of goods were falling. They wanted to get as much money for the bearskins as possible while they still could, so they sold at a reduced price. Another explanation for the term is that a bear tears its prey with its claws in a downward motion. A bull, on the other hand, goes after its opponent by pushing upward with its horns.

A bull market and a bear market are opposites of each other. The market normally moves slowly from one kind to another. Investors make more money during a bull market, and it is a symbol of a strong economy. In fact, there is a giant bronze statue of a bull prominently situated in the middle of Wall Street, very close to the NYSE.

A bull market is considered a strong, thriving market.
Stock prices rise and people make money.

## Helping the Economy

How do recessions end? Money has to be injected back into the cash-starved economy through private investments, public spending, and greater access to loans and credit. Presidents who lead during a recession often try to do something to help the economy get back on its feet and start producing again. In an attempt to end the devastating and traumatic Great Depression, US president Franklin Delano Roosevelt introduced the New Deal in the 1930s. The New Deal gave money to people who needed loans. It also introduced massive public spending and construction projects, such as the building of roads, bridges, and buildings. The project put many people back to work and eventually brought money back into the economy.

Another way to end a recession, inject cash back into a stalled economy, and stimulate upward movement in the stock market is for the government to give its citizens money to spend as they wish. During the presidency of George W. Bush, citizens received tax rebate checks that they could spend in any way they saw fit. The hope was that they would use the money to buy goods or services, putting money back into a weakening economy and stimulating it into solid growth and expansion.

During the presidency of Barack Obama, government money was given to various private organizations and state governments. This was done in order to create more jobs and prevent the country from sliding into an even deeper recession. Similar to the concept—if not the massive size—of the New Deal, President Obama's stimulus plan focused on providing jobs that might help improve the nation's roads, bridges, and buildings. It also focused on increasing green technologies. These are technologies that would help reduce our dependence on nonrenewable and environmentally harmful resources, such as fossil fuels.

When the government offers an economic stimulus, it tries to jump-start an end to a recession by giving people money in hopes that they will spend it, putting it back into the economy.

# *Funds for the Future*

Not just rich investors put their money in the stock market. Many ordinary people invest money in accounts called mutual funds. A mutual fund collects funds from a pool of people and invests it in stocks, bonds, and securities. Hopefully, these pooled investments will see a good return (i.e., make money), and the earnings are then distributed among the fund's investors. These funds are managed and traded by professional brokers.

Many people use the stock market and mutual funds to help them save for their retirement. Companies often offer their employees 401(k) accounts. These accounts put money into many different public companies so that they can grow in value before the employee retires. Individuals can also buy such accounts, called individual retirement accounts, or IRAs. The collection of shares an individual has in different companies is called his or her portfolio.

## Game of Chance

Investing in the stock market can be a risky business. In a way, it is a game of chance because the investor does not know how the company or the economy will perform over time. Some of the most successful shareholders think about how their investments will perform over the long run instead of focusing on short-term gains ("making a quick buck"). Retirement investments are often viewed this same way. In fact, the age of the investor and his or her likely retirement date is considered when 401(k) plans and IRAs are invested. Because the market has natural swings of up and down times, a young investor is encouraged to take greater risks in his or her stock choices. This will give the person a greater chance for sudden gains in profit. Investment risks (in new companies or technologies, for example) can be taken in hopes for great gains. If there are losses, the person will still have many years before retirement to make up the lost money.

As investors get older and closer to retirement, they are often advised to sell their riskier stocks and buy ones in more stable, well-established companies. Although the stock prices may not rise quickly like those of a new and untested company might, the investments are in companies that have a proven track record of consistent gains. The thought is, that during

Older people, who have less time to recover from any losses in the stock market, are often encouraged to be more conservative in their investment choices.

a slower economic time, less risky, blue chip stocks will perform more consistently than the riskier stocks of new or unproven companies. There is no guarantee that stocks will make money for the stockholder. It is even possible that older investors may lose their money—their retirement "nest egg"—right before they planned to retire and live off of it. This will mean they will have to continue working—or go back to work—at an advanced age, when they had been hoping to slow down. The security and leisure time that they had hoped to enjoy after decades of hard work and worry are suddenly taken away from them.

Companies can share their profits by selling shares, or common stock. They pay out dividends based on how well they do.

# CHAPTER 3
# *Pros and Cons of Investing*

The possibility of making money is the main reason people invest in the stock market. That possibility increases when they invest in a company that is successful and making profits. That company passes along some of the profit to shareholders by giving dividends. The dividends are usually distributed quarterly. Each company determines how much money will be given for each share of stock. Most, however, will pay less than a dollar. The more stock a shareholder has, therefore, the more dividends he or she can expect.

For example, if a shareholder owns one thousand shares of a company and the company offers a forty-cent dividend for each share, the stockholder will receive $400 each quarter. A shareholder owning less stock will receive a lower quarterly dividend. Likewise, a shareholder who owns more stock can expect higher dividends.

Dividend amounts may be increased or decreased based on the company's performance, or the company may decide not to give dividends at all. During bull markets, investors who hold shares in strongly performing companies stand to make a lot of money in dividends. This is another reason why stockholders often hold on to their shares in a company instead of constantly selling them at the first sign of a decrease in profits.

## Splitting Stocks

Sometimes stock prices may rise too high for many people to be able to afford them. Other times a company's stock prices will rise much higher than those of its competitors, making it less attractive to new investors. In response, the company's board of directors may decide to split the number of shares available for purchase. This usually means that, for every one share of stock owned, the stockholder will now have two shares of stock. The value of each share will be cut in half. This makes the price of stocks half as much as they were before, so new investors may be interested in buying into the company. They have proof that the company is successful because it just split its stock, a sure sign of strong stock market performance. And the prices have been sharply reduced per share, making investment in the high-performing company far more affordable.

Shareholders who have gone through a stock split will now have twice the number of shares they once held in the company, but the overall value of their stock will remain the same. So instead of owning one share at $10, they now own two shares at $5 each. The overall value of their stock is the same as before.

So what is the benefit of a stock split besides attracting new investors? Ultimately, the company's long-term investors will also benefit from a stock split. A new, lower price will make the stock more attractive to new investors. When they buy into the stock, the prices will be driven up. For example, if the new $5 stock goes up another dollar, the original shareholders will then have two shares at $6 each. So without investing any new money, the original shareholder now has $12 instead of $10. This rise in the stock's price may not have occurred if not for the influx of new investors. If an

# *Ground Floor Investing*

Before investing in the stock market, many investors do some research. They want to be reasonably sure that their stock will do well. So they must consider the product they are buying, the state of the industry the company is in, and the current economic times. For example, when the radio was first invented, investors bought shares of companies that manufactured radios, supplied radio parts, and produced and broadcast radio programs. But then times changed, and entertainment industry technology evolved. When television came along, there were fewer investors in radio. Investment dollars began to flow to television and its related fields.

Today, newer fields, especially green industries and computer, Internet, and information technologies, are the cutting-edge or "emerging" areas. These are areas in which investors may be able to make a large return on a relatively modest investment. The trick is to invest in smaller companies about to release an innovative breakthrough product or patent a revolutionary technology that will become the "next big thing." Once this new product or technology hits the market and generates buzz, excitement, and demand, the company's stock price will rise quickly. The stock of a start-up company may be worth $1 a share but rise to $100 share soon after a major product release. An investor who gets in early by buying ten thousand shares for $10,000 would find the same ten thousand shares suddenly worth $1 million. If the investor sold his or her shares at this point, he or she would make a $990,000 profit. That is the ultimate good return on an investment!

investor remains a shareholder for a long time, he or she may experience several splits of a stock, and his or her number of shares will keep doubling and increasing.

## Standard in the Stock Market

We can see real-life examples of how the stock market works by examining the fortunes of a few companies throughout their history. One stock market success story can be found in the oil industry. Back in the 1860s, John D. Rockefeller made a fortune building processing plants that refined petroleum. He recognized and anticipated the public demand for oil. The machines of the Industrial Revolution required oil to keep them working. People also used oil in kerosene lamps in their homes. In 1870, Rockefeller formed the Standard Oil Company, which included his refining plants. The supply of oil was great at this time, and new sources of it were being found all the time. By 1879, the Standard Oil Company controlled 90 percent of the oil market.

In the years to come, Standard Oil grew and changed many times. The company bought more and more oil fields. As far back as 1877, Standard Oil purchased another company, Vacuum Oil Company, that it thought would help it continue to grow and produce new products. The act of purchasing or obtaining another company is known as acquisition. Companies continue to do this today as a means of growing their business. It helps them expand their offerings, gain an edge over competitors, and offer their shareholders a way to make even more money.

Standard Oil continued to grow during the twentieth century, thanks in large part to the development of fuel-burning cars, trucks, buses, and airplanes. People suddenly needed oil, refined into gasoline, to transport

John D. Rockefeller (1839–1937) formed the Standard Oil Company,
a stock market success story. It offered shareholders dividends
regularly and even stock splits from time to time.

# *Funny Money?*

You already know the many ways the digital age impacts our money matters, but did you know it has sparked a new payment system and currency? Bitcoin is a virtual medium of exchange, often used for anonymous transactions. It was developed in 2009. The currency does not have a physical form—you can't put one in your pocket and take it to a local store. Users set up virtual accounts and pay for merchandise. Keep in mind that Bitcoin is highly risky to use. The Securities and Exchange Commission has kept a watchful eye on the currency and its users. For example, it has warned about the potential for the currency use in investment scams, so beware! Regarding the stock market, in May 2015, the Bitcoin Investment Trust began trading on the stock market. It is considered very risky, and investors are cautioned to only invest what they are willing to lose.

Bitcoins are a way to make payments without physical coins or bills. They can be used on many websites to buy goods and services.

themselves from place to place. There was a great demand for this resource, and shareholders made more and more money as the years went by. The company reacted to the ups and downs of the economy throughout the twentieth century. But it was successful enough to offer shareholders regular dividends and several stock splits.

## The Dot-Com Bubble

Not every public company is a stock market success story. While the oil industry became another "gold rush" in the late 1800s, so, too, did the dot-com industry in the 1990s. In the early part of the decade, the Internet was still a new, mostly unexplored world for the American public. Suddenly everyone was talking about cyberspace, the World Wide Web, and the information superhighway. It was predicted that everyone would soon have his or her own personal computer and that people would talk to each other via electronic mail and instant messaging. They would shop in virtual malls without having to leave their houses. And they could seek and find any information they needed in what amounted to the largest resource library ever to exist in human history. Needless to say, there was also a lot of money to be made in this wild frontier of a brave new cyberworld.

Start-up companies sprang up everywhere to meet this new and sudden demand for content on the Internet. Even though the information technology (IT) industry was just getting started, investors eagerly snatched up the stock of IT start-up companies. They did so even when these companies had yet to produce and market an actual product or service. Web companies with Web addresses that ended in ".com" (short for "commerce") became the recipients of millions of dollars of investors' money. Some of these companies offered little more than a ".com" in their name.

They often had no business plan, no product, and no income other than investor money.

Nevertheless, these companies felt confident that they had something to offer the public. Investors gave them millions of dollars for their initial public offering, or IPO. That means investors gave the company enough money to issue stock to the public at a certain price. A dot-com bubble occurred because people invested an incredible amount of money, often in companies that had nothing tangible to offer or sell, even after several years of investment. Stock prices were higher than they should have been. Their prices were far higher than the actual companies, their products, and their potential were worth.

Just because a company has a good idea doesn't mean that the idea will succeed. Plenty of entrepreneurs put their ideas to work during the dot-com

Some companies, like Amazon, survived the dot-com bubble's burst and still thrive today.

bubble of the late 1990s. However, by around 2001, many of them had failed and went out of business. Their investors lost thousands, and sometimes millions, of dollars. The dot-com bubble burst between 2000 and 2001. Countless start-ups had hopes of becoming the next huge company offering people popular goods and services on the Internet. When these dreams did not come true, thousands of workers were laid off. Wall Street suffered from plummeting stock prices. Investors lost millions. And the country sunk into a recession, which had an impact on the larger economy, even affecting people who did not work or invest in the IT industry.

Not every dot-com was a bust, however. Some of the companies that we now rely on and use every day to make our lives easier got their start during the era of the dot-com bubble. Google, Amazon, and eBay are all dot-com success stories. Google has changed the way people research on the Internet, and it has introduced the concept of free information with its programs Google Earth and Google Street View. Amazon and eBay have changed the way people search and shop for products. They have established new virtual markets for buying and selling. And they have found innovative ways to match sellers with buyers, allowing consumers to find even the most rare items for sale at competitive prices.

In the 1920s, inventions like movies offered joys and conveniences for Americans. Many enjoyed great prosperity, and the stock market seemed to rise with no end in sight.

# CHAPTER 4

# *The Great Depression's Effect*

How does the stock market influence everyday life? Do non-investors feel its effects? These are two important questions that often arise regarding the stock market. Know that the stock market's effect is felt in nearly every area of our lives. Its effects reach beyond investors to non-investors, regardless of age, employment status, or place of residence! This was evident in the recession of 2007–2009. A more illustrative example, however, is the Great Depression that gripped our country in the 1930s.

## Prosperity in the '20s

To fully understand that period, it helps to look at the years that came before the biggest economic downturn in US history. The 1920s were a time of great prosperity in the United States. World War I was over. There were many new inventions and technologies offering an easier life for people, including cars, refrigerators, gas stoves, telephones, radios, and even movies.

It was a time when many large companies rose and became popular with the public. The electric companies General Electric and Westinghouse, the Radio Corporation of America (RCA), and many others proved that they could make a lot of money for their investors. They inspired such confidence that more ordinary people, rather than high finance types, felt emboldened to invest their money in these corporations. For the first time, investing in the stock market became more commonplace for the average American.

The era became known as the Roaring Twenties. The stock market became a game for many Americans. People who did not even have the cash to buy stocks could still borrow money from the bank, invest, wait for their stock prices to rise, and then use some of their profits to pay back the bank loan.

This was an unusual economic time. Stock prices kept rising and rising because more and more people were investing in companies. Many newer and first-time investors did not know much about the companies they were investing in. They merely made guesses about the companies based on their names or what they thought the company produced. Everyone expected to make a profit overnight. Some stocks rose from $20 to $300 a share in just a matter of months. At this time, the average investor did not think about the risks of the stock market. There was a growing belief that the market would rise indefinitely, that there was no upper limit.

## The Crash

As the 1920s came to an end, so did the "roaring" and prosperous days of the stock market. In September 1929, stock prices began to slip. But just as soon as they fell, the prices seemed to recover themselves. Sometimes investors ended up with even more money than before after these upward surges. But as October came, dips in the market became more common, and the market seemed less of a sure thing. Investors became a bit more nervous

Confused investors wandered Wall Street after the shocking and devastating stock market crash on October 25, 1929, infamously known as Black Friday.

about the economy and less willing to pour money into stocks. People were no longer confident that their stocks were going to be a surefire way to keep making money. As people sold off their stocks and stopped investing in new ones, stock prices slipped further.

Then on Wednesday, October 23, a sudden and large rush of investors wanted to sell their stocks, all in the last hour of trading. It was a lightning-fast shock to the market. Some stock prices dropped more than $10 in that final hour, and more than two-and-a-half million shares were traded during that short time. As the closing bell rang, investors were panicked. The stock market was beginning to crash.

The next day, Thursday, October 24, the panic continued. A huge stock market crash was under way, driven largely by people's fears. Fear and panic can cause investors to pull their money out of an investment quickly and cause prices to plummet. As the New York Stock Exchange opened that morning, investors began selling immediately. There seemed to be no one willing to buy up these shares. Everyone suddenly had the same goal—dumping their stocks for any price they could. People crowded the streets in panic. By the end of the day, the total value of dumped stocks was $14 billion. That's a lot of money, even by today's standards. However, back in 1929, the figure was unbelievably large. The entire annual budget of the US government at the time was only $3 billion. Nearly five times the annual budget of the country was lost in just one day of trading.

The panic on Wall Street did not stop there. Over the next few days of trading, more and more investors sold off their stocks for increasingly low prices. "Black Tuesday," October 29, was the darkest day on Wall Street. More than $8 billion more in stock values had disappeared. From Wednesday, October 23, to Tuesday, October 29, the stock market lost more than

The collapse of the stock market meant that many banks
were stripped of much cash, causing their customers to rush
and withdraw any money left in their accounts.

$25 billion. Brokers were exhausted, some not having been home for days
because of the huge amount of paperwork that had to be filled out and filed
due to the high volume of trading.

As word spread of the stock market crash and people had less hope for its
quick recovery, insecurity about money spread from the stock market to
the banking industry. Banks had lent out a lot of money to stock market
investors. The hope was that the investor could make money in stocks and
then pay back the bank with interest. (Interest is a sort of fee charged for
borrowing money.)

## Great Losses, Great Gains

Investing in the stock market brings with it the risk of great losses on one hand and the potential for great gains on the other. The stock market crash of 1929 was devastating for investors and the economy, leading to the Great Depression. The crash caused stocks' value to drop, leading to a loss of more than $25 billion! You may have read stories about the distressing incident in which people lost their entire fortunes.

Investors don't like those types of stories. They would rather hear upbeat tales in which great gains are achieved. A recent one involves Google. On July 17, 2015, Google's stock rose 16 percent, representing a record high stock increase of $65.1 *billion*. In fact, it was the greatest one-day gain in US history! A contributing factor was the company's quarterly earnings report that exceeded economic analyst's expectations. Imagine shareholders' delight as stock values soared beyond their wildest dreams.

After the stock market collapsed, many banks were left with no money on hand. Most of it was loaned out, and there was no chance the borrowers would be able to repay it. Depositors rushed to their banks to withdraw their money, fearing that the banks would fail due to these bad loans. The banks did not have enough to hand out to everyone who wished to withdraw their money. Today, there are laws to prevent this from happening.

But back then, people lost their savings because they were left in banks that had made reckless loans. Not everyone who lost everything was a stock market investor.

## Ten Years of Economic Turmoil

The crash of 1929 was too much for the market to bounce back from. This was much more than just a brief slump in stocks. Some people who had invested their entire life savings in the stock market had lost everything during the crash. Many people dumped their stocks at bargain-basement prices or held them and watched their value plummet. Sometimes they also

When companies couldn't afford to operate, they laid off their workers and even went out of business, causing unemployment rates to rise.

lost the money they needed to pay back the banks that helped them buy those stocks in the first place.

That money had been tied up in the stock market, and it disappeared when the stock market crashed. As a result, banks failed because they could not cover the cost of those loans that would now never be repaid.

Many people had to sell all their possessions in order to raise enough money for basic necessities like clothes, food, and shelter. People sold their cars, houses, jewelry, and anything else they could get money for. Given the widespread economic collapse and suffering, though, they usually received rock-bottom prices for these valuables.

The full effects of the stock market crash would not be felt, however, for months and even years. Companies that saw their stocks plummet had little money left to operate, produce goods, or pay employees. Unemployment rose as companies went through difficult times and laid off workers. So, people who did not even have their money invested in the stock market were affected by the crash.

The country sank deeper and deeper into an economic slowdown. By 1933, one out of every four Americans was out of work. People could not meet their mortgage payments, and they lost their homes and farms. Families suffering from unemployment could not spend on consumer goods or entertainment. This caused other businesses, such as restaurants and stores, to go out of business.

As a result, even more workers were laid off. Once-wealthy businessmen were forced to sell fruit on street corners in order to make enough money to eat. People set up wooden or cardboard shelters in city parks. These shanty-towns became known as "Hoovervilles." They were named after Herbert Hoover, who was president of the United States at the time of the crash.

Hoover was roundly criticized for doing nothing to stimulate the failing economy or alleviate the suffering of millions of impoverished, hungry, unemployed, and desperate Americans.

## That Long Road to Recovery

With every economic downturn comes an eventual upturn and return to prosperity. The entire decade of the 1930s was difficult for Americans. President Roosevelt tried to fix the economy with a massive economic stimulus plan. Americans were suffering so much from the Great Depression that he promised "a new deal for the American people."

By 1933, when Franklin D. Roosevelt was elected president of the United States, circumstances were dire. His New Deal offered work and support for families in need.

The New Deal put people back to work building bridges, roads, schools, libraries, public office buildings, and other important and useful structures. This provided the families of these workers with money for life's basic necessities, like food, clothing, and shelter. In addition, the program helped improve the nation's transportation infrastructure at a time when more good, paved roads and safe and convenient bridges were desperately needed.

An important part of Roosevelt's response to the stock market crash, its causes, and the resulting Great Depression was the creation of the Securities and Exchange Commission (SEC). The SEC protects investors by monitoring and regulating the sale of stocks in the stock market. It oversees the work of stockbrokers to make sure that they are carrying out the wishes of their clients. The Federal Deposit Insurance Corporation, or FDIC, another Roosevelt creation, also protects the American people from losing money. The FDIC insures the money that people deposit into their checking and savings accounts. The government guarantees that it will cover the amount of money owed to depositors if the bank does not have the money to do so.

There was a lot of help from the government to fight the Great Depression, get Americans working and spending again, and ensure that what caused the crash would not happen again. Yet prosperity did not return to the United States until about ten years after the crash of the stock market. It was not until after America entered into World War II that the Great Depression ended.

At this time, thousands of Americans were needed to make goods for the war, such as tanks, planes, jeeps, battleships, artillery, armor, ammunition, and uniforms. Factories opened and wartime materials were produced in massive volume. Huge legions of workers—mainly women, since the young

With so many men off fighting World War II, many women stepped up to work in factories. Companies that made goods for the war effort were particularly successful.

men were off fighting the war—were put to work in factories and even on
the stock market trading floor. Stocks in companies that produced goods
for the war effort became stable and strong again.

By the time the war ended, the country had recovered from the Great
Depression. In fact, the United States had become the richest country in
the world. It was now one of only two military superpowers, along with
the Soviet Union, a wartime ally and postwar rival.

## Myths and Facts

**Myth:** No one saw the stock market crash of 1929 coming.

**Fact:** There were a few people who predicted that stock prices
could not continue to stay as high as they were. Some investors observed the dwindling money supply in banks, the huge
amount of cash lent out to investors, and the highly inflated
prices of stocks and knew that a problem was bound to arise.
They correctly saw that a slump in stock prices would result
in widespread defaults on these loans and a cash crisis for the
banks, which would not be able to cover the deposits of their
ordinary customers.

**Myth:** Everyone thought the New Deal was a good idea and
a great success.

**Fact:** There were critics of President Roosevelt who believed
that the government should not take such a strong and active

role in managing the economy. They believed that rules and regulations kept businesses from doing what they wanted to grow, expand, and make money.

**Myth:** The stock market crash was the cause of the Great Depression.

**Fact:** Many economists believe that the country was already entering a recession at the time the stock market crashed. The period of prosperity had allowed many Americans to buy goods such as cars, homes, telephones, and radios. Yet having acquired these consumer goods, the demand for the products had begun to decrease during the late 1920s. Unemployment had already been rising before the stock market crash. So it may have been the weakening economy that actually prompted the stock market crash.

# CHAPTER 5
# *Recession and the Stock Market*

---

Ever since the Great Depression, many Americans have lived in fear of a similar event rocking our nation. Although that has not happened, beginning in 2007 a recession slammed the economy and the stock market. That recession's crippling effect on our nation has been compared to the economic devastation caused by the 1929 stock market crash and the Great Depression. The downturns do have several things in common. Those similarities are helpful in understanding of what the economy and stock market endured, starting in 2007.

## Financial Real Estate Boom

During the late 1990s and first half of the 2000s, there was a financial boom in the real estate industry. It became easier and easier for people to get a mortgage (a loan to help buy a home). Normally, a mortgage is based on the income of the potential buyer, as well as the person's ability to repay the loan and his or her credit history (the person's track record of paying bills and repaying loans). Banks became more lenient and lent money to people who could not really afford the houses they bought. They didn't have enough income, and often they had poor credit histories. What's worse, banks lent them money in a way that would cause their payments to go

During the financial prosperity of the late 1990s and early 2000s, some banks became too lax about lending people more money than they would be able to pay back.

up dramatically—and sometimes unexpectedly for those homeowners who didn't read the fine print—after a few months of relatively low mortgage payments. This often put the monthly house payments beyond the range of the new homeowners.

This poor lending practice is sometimes referred to as "predatory lending." It was ignored by bank regulating authorities, mainly because home prices kept rising along with demand, and banks kept making more and more profits. No one wanted to stem this rising tide of seeming prosperity.

Construction workers enjoyed the boom in new home building. Banks enjoyed the flood of new customers. The stock market enjoyed the rising profits and stock prices of banks, mortgage lenders, and other financial institutions. All of this freewheeling lending and spending and building and buying occurred in part because the government's central bank, the Federal Reserve, was being especially hands-off. It was not carefully monitoring or regulating the business practices of many lenders and other financial institutions.

## Stock Market Slip

Buyers in over their heads, reckless lenders, and a lax and inattentive federal government all played a role in creating the housing bubble and the economic crisis that followed its bursting. In late 2008, a stock market crash alerted the country to the trouble that had been brewing for more than a year. Starting on October 6, 2008, the stock market slipped into an eight-day slide and collapse of stock prices. During that same period, the Dow Jones Industrial Average lost 22 percent of its value, or about 2,400 points. The market was very shaky for a period after that, sometimes gaining a little bit of value back, only to lose even more over the next couple of days.

At the same time that stocks were tanking, many people who were given subprime mortgages were defaulting on their payments, and banks were foreclosing on their homes. This meant the people had to move out of their homes, which would be seized and sold off by the banks that had issued their mortgages. The banks now owned the homes, so they kept any money raised by their sale. Nevertheless, because they had made so many reckless loans that would not be repaid, the banks could no longer cover all the deposits made by their checking and savings account customers. Banks began to fail, and mortgage companies entered a crisis. In some cases, the government had to step in and use money from the Federal Reserve to cover bank losses. Billions of dollars were lost by these banks and mortgage companies about a month before the stock market crashed.

In late 2008, consumers all over the United States were worried about the economy and started keeping a close eye on their spending, even on essentials.

## Economic Decline Continues

Meanwhile, more and more people lost their homes. Bank failures left banks unable to lend money to average citizens and companies that needed loans. Consumers stopped spending. Companies were forced to lay off workers. Less money went into the economy. The cycle of economic decline sped up quickly.

By 2009, most Americans were affected in some manner. Problems now existed in sectors other than the mortgage and banking industries. Unemployment rose to nearly 10 percent around the country. Although it was not as severe as the downturn of the 1930s, the financial crisis facing the country was similar to the one that occurred during the Great Depression.

The economic situation of 2009 was an eerie echo of the 1930s,
as banks closed and businesses failed.

With a poor economy comes hard times. Small businesses failed because they could not get loans from banks to continue their operations. Larger companies and state and federal governments were forced to cut their budgets to make up for lost revenue.

The financial difficulties of the United States also affected the rest of the world because the United States does so much business with companies around the globe. Cutbacks in production and reduced overseas demand for US products translated into fewer exports. The collapse in American consumer spending translated into fewer imports. As a result, both American and international companies experienced a sales slump and

People also suffered in 2009, with job cuts sending them in droves to job fairs in hopes of finding employment.

laid off workers, further reducing consumer spending. Economies around the world suffered. So did the stock prices of US and foreign companies. The recession that began with the burst bubble in the American housing industry had gone global.

## Expect the Unexpected

The stock market is vital to a country's economy—and vice versa. Anything that affects companies, people, and governments will reach back in some way to impact the economy and the stock market. This includes everything from recessions, epidemics like the 2015 Ebola medical crisis, and catastrophic weather conditions like wildfires in California.

Tragic airline crashes such as those in Malaysia in 2015, for example, also cut into company profits. Companies must find monies for replacing aircraft and pay for personal injury lawsuits that usually arise after such incidents. Profits, in turn, are impacted by consumer confidence, which usually dips after such tragedies and compels people to fly competitor airlines or temporarily stop traveling altogether. Stock prices of involved companies also plunge during such times and may cause the overall stock market to take significant hits. In turn, investors lose money. The bottom line: investing is risky, made more so because investors need to expect the unexpected!

## Protection From Recession's Harsh Effects

Just as the United States slid into a financial crisis, Americans were choosing a new commander in chief. The new president, Barack Obama, was faced with the tough decision of how to fix the economy. Should the federal government stay out of economic policy, as some economists suggest, and let market forces correct the problems? Or should the government attempt to reverse the economic free fall and protect its citizens from the harshest effects of the recession?

Part of the reason why people voted for Barack Obama was because he had expressed a strong determination to be active and aggressive in his attempts to revive the economy. On January 28, 2009, the House of Representatives approved an $819 billion economic recovery plan. It would take time for the money to be fully distributed.

It was anticipated that it would take even longer to tell if the spending plan worked and helped reverse the recession. However, within months, it was clear the plan worked. By June 2009, economists agree, the recession was over and the economy was showing signs of sustainable recovery! Among other areas in the economy beneficially impacted were unemployment, gasoline prices, the housing market, the retail sector, and consumer credit. For example, of the 8.7 million jobs lost during the recession, all have been recovered. In some cases, however, many people are still not working in the field they were prior to the downturn. In July 2007, gas prices had soared to more than $4 per gallon in areas. By mid–September 2015, the price was closer to $2–3 throughout most of the United States, with some cities boasting prices lower than $2.

If elected, Obama promised to have an aggressive approach to economic revival. In 2009 the House of Representatives approved an economic recovery plan that did help some areas of the economy.

Slammed by the recession, the housing market experienced record levels of foreclosures. Thanks in part to measures to stem predatory lending practices, the housing market has recovered. Similarly, the retail sector was hit hard by the recession as evidenced by the number of workers laid off and the number of large retail chains closing local stores. By September 2015, those ill effects of the recession had ended.

Prior to the recession, consumers had ready access to loans and credit, albeit sometimes with unaffordable and/or unclear payback terms. During the height of the recession, banks and other lenders tightened their lending practices making it difficult for consumers to receive credit, including mortgages and other loans, as well as credit cards. Additionally, many mortgages went into default because of consumers' inability to pay loans due to job loss, pay freezes and/or pay cuts. The result: record levels of foreclosures and individuals and families losing their homes. Other homeowners experienced record drops in the value of their homes. That is no longer the case, as the credit market continues to approve. Additionally, on a related front, President Obama proposed developing a new agency to help protect consumers. The Consumer Financial Protection Bureau opened in July 2011 and remains a sign that the United States will no longer allow consumers to fall prey to questionable financial practices that adversely affect citizens in any economic environment.

There will always be ups and downs in the stock market. There will be winners and losers. The same people who are winners one day can become losers the next day. People who once thought they lost it all in the stock market can suddenly find that they have made a fortune. The same risk that drives some people away from this kind of money investment can attract others.

A financial adviser can answer your questions about the stock market and help you figure out how to invest your money wisely

# Ten Great Questions to Ask a Financial Adviser

1 What can a financial adviser do for me and my savings?

2 Should I invest my money myself, or should I use a financial adviser?

3 My parents have an account called a 529 to help pay for my college tuition. What is this?

4 How much of my savings should I invest in the stock market?

5 When I research a company before buying stock, what should I try to find out about the company?

6 Should I sell my stock during a recession, or downturn, in the economy?

7 Should I take advice from other people who tell me what kind of stocks to buy?

8 Should I check the price of my stock every day?

9 Is it better to buy stocks in companies that are brand new or that have been around for a long time?

10 What should I do with the profits I make from the stock market?

Richard Cordray was appointed by President Barack Obama to head the the Consumer Financial Protection Bureau. The CFPB protects consumers from fraud and other sketchy financial practices.

The stock market is not always a hair-raising roller-coaster ride, characterized by dramatic peaks and stomach-churning drops. The general trend of the stock market over the last two hundred years and more has been a solid and steady upward swing, with occasional—and occasionally steep—setbacks. Over time, most investors see a healthy return on their investments, usually far outstripping the interest that money can earn in a savings account. Investors must be aware of the risks, research their investments, invest only a portion of their savings, and spread their money around to many different companies to minimize the chance of sudden huge losses. If they do these things, investing in the stock market can be a fairly reliable and effective way to increase personal wealth, support American corporations, and keep the economy humming.

With demand for new houses far surpassing the supply, bidding wars begin, with many people willing to pay far more than a house is worth!

# CHAPTER 6
# *The Stock Market Today*

W hat does the economy look like today, years after the last catastrophic recession? How has the stock market responded to the economy? The economy has bounced back from the recession of 2007–2009. The housing market mentioned in chapter five has rebounded. Home sales have increased. However, the prices of homes also are up. Further, the demand in some markets outpaces supply, with more buyers interested in a limited amount of properties. The result? Bidding wars for homes, with people paying much more than the sales price! Can you imagine someone paying more than the seller asks for a home?

## Getting Involved

The book describes what a stock market is and how it works. By now it is hopefully clear that the stock market affects our everyday lives. Nonetheless, it may be difficult for students to grasp this, especially if you have not experienced the stock market up close. Here are ways for you to gain firsthand knowledgeable about investing and the stock market.

One way is to play games. You may be familiar with Monopoly, which is a fun board game that allows players to buy and sell property while learning

Games can be a fun way to learn about how the stock market works. Monopoly is a well-known game, but check out others like Stock Market Game.

the ups and downs of particular financial decisions. It remains a useful tool for learning about real estate investing. Another is the Stock Market Game, a virtual investing game usually played by schools but also available to non-academic teams (including families). It gives each player $100,000 in virtual cash and encourages them to build strong investment portfolios, providing a foundation for wise real-world investing later in life. Learn more about the game at http://www.stockmarketgame.org.

Attending an investment camp is a second option for hands-on investment knowledge. These vary in duration and instruction. Each strives to equip campers with information related to financial literacy, including investing. Some include trips to local stock exchanges, a great opportunity to see stockbrokers in action. Some are hosted by local colleges, so check out your area to see if there is one that interests you.

A third way students can learn more about the stock market is to join an investment club. As its names hints, an investment club helps members join together and make investment decisions. Clubs vary in membership require-ments, so check out several before selecting one. Information about such clubs and their benefits can be found at http://www.fool.com/investment club/investmentclub01.htm.

Investing in the stock market is an effective fourth method for develop-ing your stock market know-how. Do some research into the companies that interest you and talk to your parents about your plans. (Be sure to get permission from your parents are guardians before investing.) You can start small by opening an account and buying one or a few stocks in companies that you are familiar with or that have products that you enjoy. Starting with just one share is affordable, especially if you use money received from special occasions or from a part-time job.

## Around the World

Some global economies are experiencing weak growth and high unem-ployment even as the US economy remains stronger. Greece and China have both experienced recent stock market crises. China's economic woes shifted its bull market into a bear one in summer 2015.

In 2010, Greece faced near bankruptcy. It received two financial bailouts in order to improve its economy and avoid bankruptcy. By 2015, the coun-try experienced increased financial problems. As the crisis unfolded, many fearful Greek citizens withdrew money from banks. To stem the impact on

One way to learn about the stock market is to jump right in and start investing. It can be as easy as using an app on your smartphone.

When their country was near bankruptcy in 2015,
Greek citizens voted against receiving a third economic bailout.

banks, the government implemented various measures, including temporarily closing banks and limiting how much money citizens could withdraw. To improve the economy, including the stock market and banking industry, Greece received emergency financial help in July 2015.

Meanwhile, much to the shock of many investors worldwide, China's stock market crashed on August 24, 2015, impacting the US and other global markets. Stock value losses were tremendous. The crash came on the heels of a year-long bull market during which stock prices steadily increased. After the crash, the Chinese government implemented measures to reverse the

# *Digital Footprints*

Stock market information is closer than you think. Pull down the iPhone's main screen, for example, and you'll see stock price information for various companies. Computer-based apps provide digital information as well.

Use apps on your smartphone, tablet, or laptop to learn more about recession or other issues affecting the economy. Some apps cover more technical topics specific to the economy and how it works. Personal finance apps are more user-friendly, providing information on spending, budgeting, and investing. Apps you may learn from now and use later include mortgage calculators, debt reduction calculators, and currency convertors.

Stock prices and other information may be right at your fingertips. Some smartphones and tablets have that information one swipe away from the main screen.

decline. Investor confidence, however, had already been negatively affected. China's stock market continued to be volatile.

Greece and China's financial problems show how the stock market is impacted by a country's economy. A strong, flourishing economy helps the stock market, while a weak, faltering economy hurts the stock market—and vice versa.

## End of Bull Run?

The stock market has experienced some highs and lows, but overall a bull market is prevailing. In fact, Since March 2009, the United States has been in the midst of the longest bull market since the Great Depression!

The stock market has been experiencing a bull run since 2009, but it experiences downturns from time to time. Just keep watching and see if it will go up again.

Investment professionals, anticipating that the bull has to run out of steam at some point, are cautioning investors to expect a bear market in the future. Mixed predictions prevail concerning how long the bull market will last. Some analysts predict it may end anytime soon, while others predict that, given the current economic conditions, it may last for years. Only time will tell!

# Stock Market Timeline

---

**1685** Wall Street in New York built, later becomes known as the US financial center.

**1792** First formal New York stock exchange created when twenty-four stockbrokers sign the Buttonwood Agreement.

**1817** The New York Stock and Exchange Board is created.

**1863** The organization's name is changed to the New York Stock Exchange (NYSE).

**1867** Ticker tape machine invention provides simultaneous market information to brokerage houses.

**1892** NYSE organizes itself to facilitate broker transactions.

**May 26, 1896** Dow Jones Industrial Average created.

**July 31, 1914–November 1914** NYSE closes because of World War I.

**1920s** Roaring Twenties era, a prosperous time for the stock market.

**October 24, 1929** Stock market crashes, sparks the Great Depression.

**1934** SEC created to protect investors and regulate stock sales.

**1957** Standard & Poor's 500 (S&P) created.

**1971** National Association of Securities Dealers Automated Quotations (NASDAQ) created.

**1987** Black Monday stock market crash; stock falls more than 22 percent.

**2000–2001** Dot.com bubble bursts; investors lose millions.

**September 11, 2001** NYSE and the NASDAQ do not open after news of terrorist attacks on 9/11.

**September 17, 2001** NYSE and the NASDAQ reopen; stock values drop.

**2007** Real estate bubble bursts, sparking the Great Recession.

**July 7, 2015** NYSE stops trading for almost four hours due to technology glitch.

# Bibliographic Resources

Bair, Sheila. *The Bullies of Wall Street: This Is How Greed Messed Up Our Economy.* New York: Simon & Schuster Children's Publishing Division, 2015.

Blumenthal, Karen. *Six Days in October: The Stock Market Crash of 1929.* New York, NY: Atheneum Books for Young Readers, 2002.

Calmes, Jackie. "House Passes Stimulus Plan with No GOP Votes." *The New York Times,* January 28, 2009. Retrieved September 2009 (http://www.nytimes.com/2009/01/29/us/politics/29obama.html).

Cendrowski, Scott. "China's Stock Market Crashes Again as Panicking Sellers Lose Faith." *Fortune,* July 27, 2015. Retrieved September 11, 2015 (fortune.com/2015/07/27/china-stock-market-crashes-again-with-panic-selling/).

Chatzky, Jean. *Not Your Parents Money Book.* New York: Simon & Schuster Children's Publishing Division, 2010.

CNNMoney.com. "The Bull Market Lives: Stocks Rise 11.4% in 2014." December 31, 2014. Retrieved September 11, 2015 (http://money.cnn.com/2014/12/31/investing/stocks-market-2014-great-year/).

Curran, Rob. "A Bitcoin Fund Is Born, With Teething Pains." *The Wall Street Journal*, July 7, 2015.

ExxonMobil. "Our History." ExxonMobil, 2015. Retrieved October 28, 2015 (http://corporate.exxonmobil.com/en/company/about-us/history/overview).

Fraser, Steve. *Wall Street: America's Dream Palace*. New Haven, CT: Yale University Press, 2008.

German, Kent. "Top 10 Dot-com Flops." CNet. Retrieved June 2009 (http://www.cnet.com/1990-11136_1-6278387-1.html).

Hope, Bradley, Strump Dan, and Vaishampayan Saumya. "Glitch Freezes Big Board." *The Wall Street Journal*, July 9, 2015.

Kapner, Hope. "Gap to Close a Quarter of Its US Stores." *The Wall Street Journal*, June 16, 2015.

Kent, Zachary. *The Story of the New York Stock Exchange* (Cornerstones of Freedom). Chicago, IL: Children's Press, 1990.

Krantz, Matt. "Google Mints Record $65B in Wealth in a Day." *USAToday.com*, July 17, 2015. Retrieved September 11, 2015 (http://americasmarkets.usatoday.com/2015/07/17/google-mints-record-65b-in-wealth-in-a-day/).

Money-zine.com. "Stock Market Crash of 2008." Money-Zine, 2008. Retrieved June 2009 (http://www.money-zine.com/Investing/Stocks/Stock-Market-Crash-of-2008).

*New York Times.* "Economic Stimulus: Latest Developments." June 26, 2009. Retrieved July 2009 (http://topics.nytimes.com/topics/reference/ timestopics/subjects/u/united_states_economy/economic_stimulus).

Peter, Ian. "History of the Internet: The Dot-com Bubble." NetHistory .com. Net History, 2004. Retrieved June 2009 (http://www.net history.info/History%20of%20the%20Internet/dotcom.html).

Practical Small Business Information. "What Caused the 2008 Recession?" Practical Small Business Info, 2008. Retrieved June 2009 (http:// practicalsmallbusiness.info/recession/what-caused-the-2008-recession).

Schoen, John. "Is This Another Great Depression?" MSNBC, January 21, 2009. Retrieved June 2009 (http://www.newsvine .com/_news/2009/01/21/2340049-is-this-another-great-depression).

SEC.gov. "The Investor's Advocate: How the SEC Protects Investors, Maintains Market Integrity, and Facilitates Capital Formation." US Securities and Exchange Commission, 2013. Retrieved June 2009 (http://www.sec.gov/about/whatwedo.shtml).

Securities and Exchange Commission. *Investor Alert: Ponzi Schemes Using Virtual Currencies.* July 1, 2013. Retrieved September 15, 2015 (www.sec.gov/investor/alerts/ia_virtualcurrencies.pdf).

Smith, Aaron. "Madoff's Day of Reckoning." CNN.com, June 29, 2009. Retrieved June 2009 (http://money.cnn.com/2009/06/26/news/ economy/madoff_sentence/index.htm).

*The Washington Post Express.* "Google Posts Record 1-day Windfall of $65.1B." "Weekend Rewind" section, July 20, 2015, p. 45.

Whitcrafe, Melissa. *Wall Street* (Cornerstones of Freedom). Chicago, IL: Children's Press, 2003.

Wilson, Andrew B. "Five Myths About the Great Depression." *The Wall Street Journal*, November 4, 2008. Retrieved June 2009 (http://online.wsj.com/article/SB122576077569495545.html).

# Glossary

**acquisition**—The act of buying or obtaining something.

**bear market**—A period of falling stock prices.

**bull market**—A period of rising stock prices.

**capitalism**—An economic system in which trade and industry can be privately owned, rather than government owned, and designed to make a profit for the owners.

**commodity**—A good that is sold before being processed, such as wheat, tobacco, or cotton.

**depression**—A period of prolonged and deep economic recession.

**dividend**—The amount of money paid by companies to their shareholders.

**economy**—The growth or wealth of a region or country.

**Federal Reserve**—The system of federal banks that controls the US money supply.

**foreclosure**—The process of taking away a person's property because of failure to keep up with mortgage payments.

**initial public offering (IPO)**—The first time a company sells shares of its ownership—stocks—to the public.

investor—A person who spends money on a company or enterprise and expects to make a profit in return.

portfolio—The collection of shares an individual has in different companies.

prosperity—A period of economic success, growth, and wealth.

public company—A company that sells shares of its ownership to the public.

recession—A period of economic decline.

regulation—The rules made and enforced by a governing authority.

securities—Certificates of stocks that prove a person's partial ownership of a company.

share—A unit of ownership in a company; a share of stock.

split—The breaking up or dividing of stocks in order to lower per share prices.

start-up company—A newly created company with no previous business history.

stock—A unit of ownership in a company.

subprime mortgage—A type of mortgage (loan to buy a house) given to people with low income and often poor credit ratings.

trading—The buying and selling of stocks.

# Further Reading

## Books

Bair, Sheila. *The Bullies of Wall Street: This Is How Greed Messed Up Our Economy*. New York, NY: Simon & Schuster Children's Publishing Division, 2015.

Becket, Michael. *How the Stock Market Works: A Beginner's Guide to Investment*. 4th Ed. London; Philadelphia, PA: Kogan Page, 2014.

Bernstein, Daryl. *Better Than a Lemonade Stand! Small Business Ideas for Kids*. New York, NY; Hillsboro, OR: Aladdin/Beyond Words, 2012.

Bianchi, David W. *Blue Chip Kids: What Every Child (and Parent) Should Know About Money, Investing, and the Stock Market*. Hoboken, NJ: Wiley, 2015.

Catel, Patrick. *Money and Government*. Chicago, IL: Heinemann Library, 2012.

Catel, Patrick. *Money and Trade*. Chicago, IL: Heinemann Library, 2012.

Donovan, Sandra. *Job Smarts: How to Find Work or Start a Business, Manage Earnings, and More*. Minneapolis, MN: Twenty-First Century Books, 2012.

Gagne, Tammy. *Investment Options for Teens*. Hockessin, DE: Mitchell Lane Publishers, 2014.

Levete, Sarah. *Dollars and Sense: The Banking Industry*. New York, NY: Gareth Stevens Pub., 2013.

Peterson's. *Don't Break the Bank: A Student's Guide to Managing Money*. Lawrenceville, NJ: Peterson's Publishing, 2012.

Tyson, Eric. *Investing for Dummies*. 7th Ed. Hoboken, NJ: John Wiley & Sons, 2014.

## Websites

**Bank It**

*www.bankit.com/youth*

Interactive resource helping teens discover more about financial topics with follow-up questions for talking about money with parents.

**BizKids**

*bizkids.com/themes/saving-investing*

Videos, entrepreneurship tools, games, and other resources for youth.

**Business Insider**

*www.businessinsider.com/20-under-20-in-finance-2013-11#ixzz3iBQWIjVX*

Article, "THE 20 UNDER 20: Meet The Teen Traders Trying To Take Over The Finance World."

**Savings Spree**

*www.msgen.com/assembled/savings_spree.html*

App for financial literacy game for learning about budgeting and other topics.

**Teens and Money**

*www.saveandinvest.org/FinancialBasics/Teens/*

Videos, financial calculators, posters, games, and other financial tools for teens.

**Test Your Money $marts**

*www.sec.gov/investor/tools/quiz.htm*

Brief investment-related questionnaire.


**The Mint**

*www.themint.org/teens*

Resources on various money topics, including investing, provided by Northwestern Mutual.

# Index